A GIRL'S GUIDE TO...
MAN MANAGEMENT

EVERY WOMAN'S GUIDE TO GETTING HER MAN WHERE
SHE WANTS HIM...AND KEEPING HIM THERE

D0958339

Jane Matthews

CONARI PRESS

This Edition first published in 2006 by Conari Press,
an imprint of Red Wheel/Weiser, LLC
York Beach, ME
with offices at:
500 Third Street, Suite 230
San Francisco, CA 94107
www.redwheelweiser.com

Copyright © 2006 by Axis Publishing Ltd.

Created and conceived by:
Axis Publishing Limited
8c Accommodation Road
London NW11 8ED, UK
www.axispublishing.co.uk

Creative Director: Siàn Keogh
Editorial Director: Anne Yelland
Managing Editor: Conor Kilgallon
Design: Simon de Lotz, Sean Keogh
Production: Jo Ryan, Cécile Lerbière

Library of Congress information available upon request.

Typeset in Myria by Axis Design Editions

Printed and bound in China by CT Printing
13 12 11 10 09 08 07 06
8 7 6 5 4 3 2 1

CONTENTS...

INTRODUCTION

You may not be head of your own company yet—but you are already a man manager.

Think about it. Even before you could speak you almost certainly knew how to get your own way, either by smiling or by screaming.

As you grew up you learned a wider range of emotions and techniques to bend people to your will: from pleading and persuasion on your dad when he wanted to buy you a book rather than Barbie's latest outfit, to eyelash fluttering at the boy down the street, who happened to have a bit of a crush on you—and a swimming pool in his yard.

You've also heard the saying that behind every great man is a great woman—who is able to maneuver her man to get her own way.

Eve and Adam, Cleopatra and Anthony, Hillary and Bill: there is clearly nothing new about the idea of women who function as man managers.

And thank goodness for that. Because left to themselves guys do have a tendency to mess things up.

Not just in the big, bad worlds of business and politics, but in the place where it matters even more: in their relationships with us. Your life, heart, home, future, whatever.

Do you realize there are still guys who vanish faster than inhibitions on a pub night the moment a girl says "we need to talk"? Guys who'd sooner ditch you than ditch the dishes in a washing-up bowl. Who think "G" spot is a type of

glue. And can't understand why you don't laugh when they relay crude jokes from the locker room.

Let's face it, they need all the support you can give them to be able to properly appreciate you and earn their place in your thoughts, your heart, your bed, and maybe even in the future you are planning.

That's where this book is going to help you—by helping him to be part of a great partnership.

But before we get down to the nitty gritty of how you get him to romance you in style and learn to launder his own boxer shorts (along with your underwear too), we need to sort out what we mean by man management.

If there's one thing guys say they hate above everything, it's girls who try to change them. You can see their point. You'd think twice about saying "yes" to a guy who wanted to turn you into someone else, especially if it's the ex he's still obsessed with.

So what this book is not about is forcing him to become someone he's not. There will always be a sell-by date on your love affair if one of you is trying to be happy at the expense of the other.

Nor is it an attack on men. After all, we love them to pieces (most of the time), and we realize we're not completely perfect ourselves either (apart from you, that is).

Rather, you can see it as a sort of management training manual, which will help you understand how he ticks—the way he thinks, feels, and acts—in order to bring out his true potential. After all, good managers know the difference between leadership and dictatorship.

Dictators give orders and use people in whatever way they can to get what they want, even if that means lying and deceit. They may get results but their lack of integrity and decency means that in place of love and loyalty they foster fear, resentment, and rebellion.

Leaders know the best way to earn loyalty and respect is to give it. That the quickest route to the right results is to offer generous support and training and to focus effort toward a common goal. To get the best from people they need to praise, approve, appreciate, and appreciate some more.

Perhaps you're looking for a man to love and for a relationship in which you both flourish. Or maybe you've already got the guy, but you're definitely not feeling loved, appreciated, or listened to.

So think of yourself as the CEO of a promising new business which could deliver excellent results once you acquire the know-how and skills to bring out your guy's potential.

The good news is that when you do, it's not only him, but the whole enterprise that will flourish.

WHAT DO YOU

WANT?

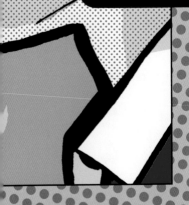

FINDING YOURSELF WITH THE WRONG GUY IS SOMETHING MOST OF US KNOW ABOUT. PAINFUL AS THIS CAN BE, THOUGH, IT HURTS EVEN MORE TO FIND YOURSELF WITH THE RIGHT GUY, BUT IN THE WRONG RELATIONSHIP. YOU LOVE EACH OTHER; EVERYONE SAYS YOU'RE GREAT TOGETHER, AND YOUR HEAD'S TELLING YOU YOU'VE GOT EVERYTHING GOING FOR YOU. BUT FOR EVERY MOMENT THINGS RUN SMOOTHLY, DAYS GO BY WHEN ONE OF YOU IS SIMMERING WITH RESENTMENT, ANGER, DISTRUST, OR PLAIN DISLIKE FOR ONE ANOTHER. IF THIS SOUNDS FAMILIAR, READ ON. . .

And they all lived happily ever after... you've heard that since before you could read, and likely were brought up believing it. But life for grown-ups goes on long after the book shuts or the credits roll.

LOVE HIM, HATE HIM

TRUTH OR MYTH?

Strong and silent may work in fairy tales, but rarely in real life. Life doesn't mirror the movies —they don't usually show much everyday reality, let alone the gritty truth of relationships. The romantic classics we grew up with stop just after the hero and heroine finally overcome the obstacles to their getting together. Think about it—in today's terms, the story stops pretty much after you first realize this counts as a relationship rather than a four-date fling. "Happy ever after" in real life is where the work of relationships begins. Try not to think in little-girl terms—accept that life's more interesting when you start to take it on as an adult.

To get what you want, you need to take charge of your own happiness. If that concept hasn't sunk in yet, it's not your fault. From the day you realized little girls and little boys were different, you've been seduced by all those books, movies, and TV scripts—fiction in other words—to believe that requited love is the end of the story and that once you reach happy-ever-after there's nothing more than an optimistic "The End" to believe in.

Except that in real life there's always a morning after. And however good a match your man appears to be, mismatched expectations, ideas, and behavior will lead to you waking up and realizing that, far from happy-ever-after, you're going to find your life together frustrating, exasperating, or just plain impossible.

If love were enough, none of us would ever have a dud relationship or break up with the partner we fell in love with. But to want to be with someone every Saturday night for 52 weeks of the year, and to happily wake up next to them every Sunday morning, the glue of a relationship has to be stronger and last longer than that just-got-together feeling, or even than really great sex.

You have to be getting what you need from the relationship—and so does he. Otherwise, when in-love or in-lust fades to in-doubt, you'll suddenly find that there's no deeper layer of reasons for you two to stay together and go the relationship distance.

It's not his responsibility to realize what you want and give it to you—it's yours to help him to understand your needs so that he can meet them.

HE DOESN'T REALLY NEED MANAGING, DOES HE?

It doesn't matter how lavish the gesture, the biggest compliment your guy can pay you is knowing you well enough to give you the right gift every time—the one that brings tears (of pleasure!) to your eyes.

CHLOE'S STORY...

Chloe is the envy of all her friends because she's with a gorgeous, talented, sensitive guy who thinks she's a goddess. She and Mike have been together for a while and he's still convinced she can do no wrong—so much so that he'd do anything to please her.

To prove it, Mike threw a huge party to celebrate her last birthday and, when the speeches were over, led Chloe and their guests outside to see his present for her—a gleaming two-seater sports car with a creamy leather interior.

All the guys were speechless, torn between envy and fear that their girlfriends would expect a similarly outrageous gesture from them.

For most of the girls, though—including Chloe—it wasn't such an awesome gift. What it was, actually, was the sort of gift Mike would have loved to receive himself. And what was running through Chloe's head as she thanked him a little too profusely was, how would she carry the week's shopping home in it? Or take her sister's two kids to the zoo? And would her friends and colleagues think that she was being showy when she roared up in her new wheels?

Mike's gift could lead to all sorts of problems, with Chloe feeling hurt or cross that after all this time he still doesn't understand her enough to know she isn't the fast car type, and Mike growing resentful that, though he's spent a fortune trying to please her, she insists on keeping her trusty old Chevy and using it often.

Man management means making sure that your guy knows, whether you put it in words or not, that the gesture that would really make you go weak at the knees is coffee in bed each day—before he wastes his money on a car that reflects his dream and not yours.

HOW TO SHORTEN THE ODDS

Before you start to manage your man, you need to be sure that he really is a good fit for what you want; don't waste your energy on a guy who, ultimately, is never going to match up to your standards.

First things first. You've heard the expression about not being able to turn a sow's ear into a silk purse.

Before you start to put your time and energy into management, make sure you've got the right raw material. Decide which are the areas in which you can give a little, and which are those in which you're not prepared to compromise.

This is where his resume needs to be a good fit for your job description. He's allowed a few gaps in his background, because you've proved, by buying this book, that you're willing to invest in a bit of on-the-job training.

But if he's lacking any of your true essentials, you really will be wasting your time, setting you both up to fail.

The following pages give you a fun way of trying to establish in your own mind what you're looking for in a guy. Most of us tend to wait until we've fallen in love before considering whether he's right for us. Or we convince ourselves that because we're in love we'll put up with what we get.

Drawing up a template for your ideal man doesn't mean you have to dismiss anyone who isn't a prefect fit. But if you understand yourself well, you're more likely to choose wisely in the first place.

FALL IN LOVE WITH YOUR EYES OPEN! THE BETTER YOU UNDERSTAND YOURSELF AND WHAT YOU NEED, THE LESS LIKELY YOU ARE TO SUFFER FROM SHORT SIGHT WHEN IT COMES TO YOUR PARTNER.

DRAWING UP THE BLUEPRINT

Through life's ups and downs you're looking for a guy who can make the ups even better and the downs bearable. Try this exercise to help you to refine the qualities your ideal guy has to have.

For years, men have had it their way with fantasies about finding a girl who'll be a whore in the bedroom, servant in the home, and trophy on their arm. Now it's your turn to imagine your ideal man, bringing together as many of the guys you've dreamed of as you like.

Imagine you are designing your perfect partner. Think about each of these situations, then write down the name of the guy you'd choose to share them with. He can be anyone: celebrity, fictional character, someone from history, someone you know—if you're lucky, he may even be in your life already. Then, under each scenario, write down what qualities or characteristics this guy has that made you choose him—and use the answers you arrive at to draw up a personalized wishlist for the perfect partner for you.

WHO IS HE?

It's your best friend's wedding and everyone you know will be there. Who do you want to join you?
*Name*_____

Characteristics _____
_____

Your mom wants you to bring your guy home for Thanksgiving but you know your relatives are eccentric (verging on the lunatic). Who will you bring?
*Name*_____

Characteristics _____
_____

You're stuck in bed with flu, your nose is crimson, your eyes are swollen, and you're in a rotten mood. Who do you want to look after you?

Name_____

Characteristics _____
_____

It's a week to pay day and you're too poor to buy food for you or the cat. Who's the generous benefactor you long to see at your door?

Name_____

Characteristics _____
_____

Your boss has invited you—and a male friend—to join him at a smart dinner. There'll be more diamonds and tony accents than on the Titanic. Who will you ask?

Name_____

Characteristics _____
_____

You've just watched a sexy moment in your favorite TV series and the shiver in your belly says it's time to switch off so he can turn you on. Who do you want sitting beside you?

Name_____

Characteristics _____
_____

Can you see a pattern emerging? Now read on...

With the right mix of raw materials reflecting both your "must-have" and "desirable" characteristics, your helping hand can guide your man a long way toward meeting your criteria, but there are some things that can't be taught.

ESSENTIALS & DESIRABLES

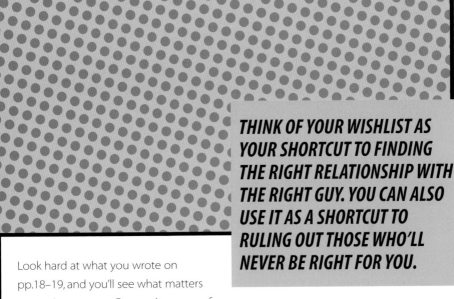

THINK OF YOUR WISHLIST AS YOUR SHORTCUT TO FINDING THE RIGHT RELATIONSHIP WITH THE RIGHT GUY. YOU CAN ALSO USE IT AS A SHORTCUT TO RULING OUT THOSE WHO'LL NEVER BE RIGHT FOR YOU.

Look hard at what you wrote on pp.18–19, and you'll see what matters to you in a partner. Generosity, sense of humor, patience, drop-dead-gorgeous looks, even a weird family of his own: your list will be as individual as you.

But before you commit this list to memory, so you can check whenever you think a guy shows promise, make sure you're clear about which items on your list it would be nice to find— "desirable" in resumé language—and which are absolute non-negotiables.

Another way of looking at what you want is to consider what's already working for you. We meet hundreds, even thousands of people in our lifetimes, but we only choose to turn some of them into friends. Usually

they've got some of the characteristics on both our desirable and our essential lists: they make us feel good about ourselves, we enjoy their company, we may even want to be like them.

Are you after someone who can show you a good time, someone to curl up with, someone who needs you as much as you need them, or all of those things? Have you prioritized your wishlist to see what you want most?

Do you like to think your relationships are going somewhere (even as far as up the aisle) or will you be happy for a time with someone who's Mr Right-For-Now?

NATURE VERSUS PERSONALITY

There's a lot you can do in terms of management to get what you want and need from your man and your relationship—but be careful not to confuse who he appears to be with who he really is.

If Mike had really wanted to turn Chloe into grateful mush, he should have kept his credit card in his top pocket and brought her hand-picked flowers every day for a week.

But at least Mike wanted to please Chloe. He wanted to make a public statement of his love and commitment to her. And generosity and thoughtfulness are just two of the things that can't be taught—and that are likely to come quite high on your wishlist. So before you embark on an intensive course to teach your man to express his feelings and to give you the warmth you need, do ensure that the man you're teaching has the basic underlying qualities (and they can be buried quite deep) that make him worth working with.

Over the space of your love affair you can teach him how to express his love for you, but you can't teach him to be loving if he's actually all for show. If that's the case you'll find that he'll quickly master the lines, but he'll never really mean them.

You can't teach him to be enthusiastic about the things that mean a lot to you—kicking leaves in a park, watching old movies, collecting labels from jelly jars, whatever you like doing that makes you feel good—if he lacks the ability to empathize with you and, although you can use chapter three to help turn him into a great lover, if he's actually too self-centered to care all that much about feelings rather than technique, it'll only ever be text-book sex.

AIMING HIGH—OR IN CLOUD-CUCKOO LAND?

If he ticks all the boxes on your wishlist, you've found the right guy in the right relationship at the right time—but even if he doesn't, take a reality check yourself to be sure you are not asking for the impossible.

While you're thinking about what matters to you in a man, here are a few things to remember.

LIKE THE MAN SAID, MEN REALLY ARE FROM MARS...

Look down your list of essentials. Chances are, your best girlfriends would already rate a tick in most of the boxes but you've not yet met the guy who does. Difference DOES make life more difficult, but it also makes it richer and more challenging and, when you get it right, more exciting and rewarding. Remember, managing your man isn't about turning him into a male version of you and your female friends. It's about understanding how—and to a certain extent why—he's different and then using that knowledge to your own advantage!

NOBODY'S PERFECT

You deserve the very best; there's nothing wrong with having high standards. But do make sure you've still kept a toehold in real life. It's important that you don't raise your expectations to the level where nobody can fulfill them. We'd all love to wake up next to our movie hero or our fairy-tale knight. Asking for a guy to be strong, capable, principled, cute, a great lay, brilliant with kids and animals, and prepared to get us out of any global emergency that may arise is fine. But those heroes aren't real, and they don't live in the real world where you can meet and date them. (Ask yourself, if you're getting too picky, how well you measure up to the fairy-tale/movie heroine yourself. Remind yourself that your man may have a few boxes of his own to tick.)

BE SURE YOU REALLY WANT WHAT YOU'RE ASKING FOR

Think about how you'd feel if your man suddenly started displaying the qualities you dream of. If you wish he'd shed a tear at a sad movie sometimes, instead of loudly denouncing it as girl stuff, imagine how you'd feel if he wept copiously all the way home. Not such a good picture? Empathy, honesty, and a soft center: all good things. But you want to be sure that they aren't just neediness in disguise.

WHO ARE

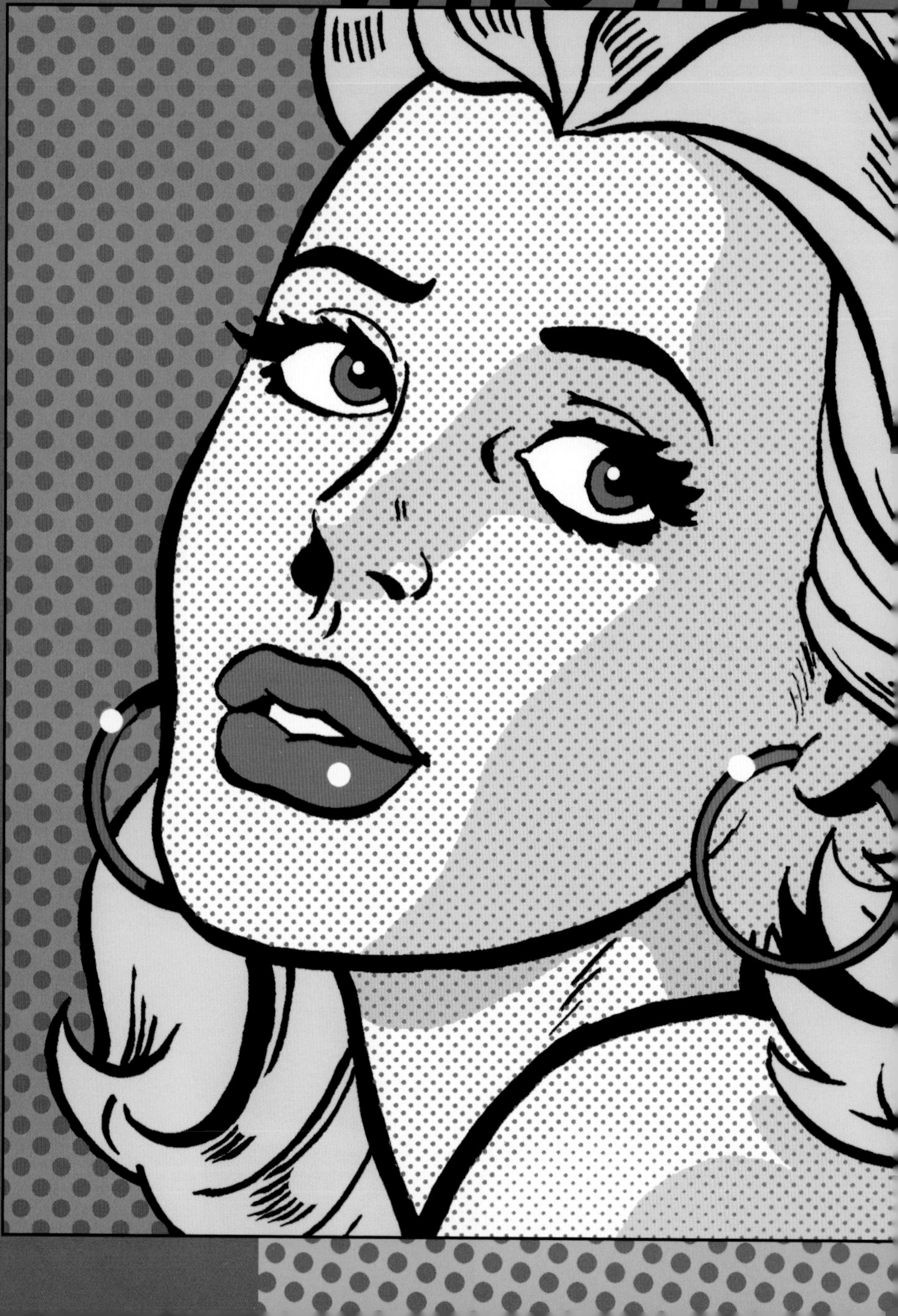

YOU?

WE LIKE TO KNOW OUR IDOLS HAVE BAD HAIR DAYS. YOU KNOW THE SORT OF BLURRY PAPARAZZI SHOTS: WORLD-CLASS STARS SHUFFLING ALONG THE SIDEWALK IN BAGGY PANTS AND SCUFFED SNEAKERS. WHEN WE SEE SOMEONE THAT FAMOUS LOOKING BAD, IT SOMEHOW GIVES US PERMISSION TO SPORT THE OCCASIONAL ZIT. ACTUALLY YOU'RE MISSING THE POINT HERE. THE BEAUTIFUL PEOPLE KNOW WHAT THEY'RE DOING WHEN THEY OPT FOR A DRESS-DOWN DAY. IT'S PRECISELY BECAUSE THEY DON'T WANT TO STAND OUT FOR THE CAMERAS THAT THEY LEAVE OFF THE MAKE-UP, SHRUG ON THE SLOPPIES, AND ADOPT THE BODY LANGUAGE OF SOMEONE THE DOG WOULD THINK TWICE ABOUT DRAGGING IN. IT'S VERY EASY TO BECOME INVISIBLE IF YOU DRESS AND ACT LIKE SOMEONE WITH ZERO SELF-ESTEEM.

LEARN TO PLAY
THE CONFIDENCE TRICK

It may be fine for really big stars to dress down, but what about you? Do you sometimes feel as if you must be wearing a cloak of invisibility? Do you feel that no-one pays you any attention, or sees you for what you are?

Do you believe you're "worth it"? Or are you too busy apologizing for using up oxygen ever to challenge the guy in your life? Your thought process runs something like this: "I'm lucky to have him. I've got to put up with his horrible personal habits and the offhand way he treats me because if I complain he'll go and find someone who doesn't."

Actually, he won't. If he does leave you it's more likely to be because he's met a girl who wears her self-esteem on her sleeve and won't stand for such nonsense—she knows exactly how lucky he is to have her! We all feel good around people who feel good about themselves: the trouble with doormats is that they quickly get shabby from everyone walking all over them. Behave as if you're the last word in quality and people will believe it. Conversely, most

people are too busy to take the trouble to find out how fantastic you are if you don't bother to show it.

To tackle his shortcomings you need to feel confident that you're definitely a good catch and he's lucky you're willing to make the effort.

Self-esteem means that you must give yourself all the things that you're willing to give your guy: love, approval, trust, and respect. Use the way that you treat yourself to set an example to others of how they should treat you. Sooner or later you will start to believe your own publicity…because it's true.

An independent woman who knows she can manage without her man has the best chance of keeping him. Take a look at the exercise on pp. 30–31 to see whether you place yourself top of the pile, or by the exit.

29

SO WHAT DO YOU THINK YOU'RE WORTH?

Forget PMS. What many girls suffer from most is low self-esteem. This exercise will help you to see whether your ring of confidence is really there, or whether you're just putting on an act.

GOLD, SILVER, OR BRONZE?

Think hard about each of these statements and tick those that ring true for you.

1 If I fight with a guy I think he'll leave me. ☐

2 I feel as if my relationships with men are only as strong as the last time we were together. ☐

3 If a date goes badly I don't expect him to call me again. ☐

4 I've sometimes stayed with a guy because I didn't think I'd find anyone else. ☐

5 At work, I'm waiting for someone to find out I'm not up to the job. ☐

6 I put in a lot of extra effort to show my boss s/he can't afford to lose me. ☐

7 I feel a fraud when people treat me as if I know what I'm talking about. ☐

8	*I usually think other people are more successful than me.*	☐
9	*When people pay me compliments I think they're just saying that to be nice.*	☐
10	*A lot of the time I feel unhappy about my appearance.*	☐
11	*I try very hard to make people like me.*	☐
12	*I find it hard to ask people to do things for me.*	☐
13	*I find it even harder to say no when they ask me to do something I don't want to.*	☐
14	*I often settle for what I can get, rather than what I want.*	☐

HOW DID YOU DO?

Fewer than four ticks: Gold
You know your worth and your shiny self-esteem brings people flocking. You should have no trouble helping the guys in your life become worthy of you.

Between four and eight: Silver
Your self-esteem is like silver. When you find the energy and inclination to polish it up you sparkle. But all too often you neglect it and the gleam of your true value is hidden under layer on layer of dull tarnish.

More than eight: Bronze
We see bronze as for also-rans. But don't despair: our ancestors rated bronze more highly than other metals because it was both practical and decorative. So polish up your act and let your value shine through.

WHAT ARE YOU LIKE?

Low self-esteem packs a double punch: you don't value yourself enough to believe that you deserve what you want from life, and that makes you behave in ways that just add to the dislike you feel for yourself.

Remember when you were a child and didn't get what you wanted (or even how you reacted last week when you thought someone was criticizing you)?

Instead of feeling secure enough to respond in a direct way, to stand up for yourself, you're liable to adopt a whole lot of other, less direct and often even unattractive behaviors.

Simmering resentment, sulking, moaning, and nagging are all tactics that many women have a habit of dragging from the barrel if we feel others aren't doing right by us.

If you're guilty of this it's because, deep down, you don't believe you deserve the best. So you're quick to take offense, and to read criticism or disapproval into the things your guy says or does, when he probably meant nothing at all by them.

Other dubious tactics to get your own way include punishing him with silence, using emotional blackmail, acting cold, withdrawing sex, or even starting a campaign of criticism to ensure he feels bad about himself. All of which adds up to the definitive guide to how NOT to get what you want.

So here's another reason it makes sense to work on your self-esteem as well as your man management skills: if you don't you'll end up blaming him all the more, not just for failing to deliver but for "making" you behave badly.

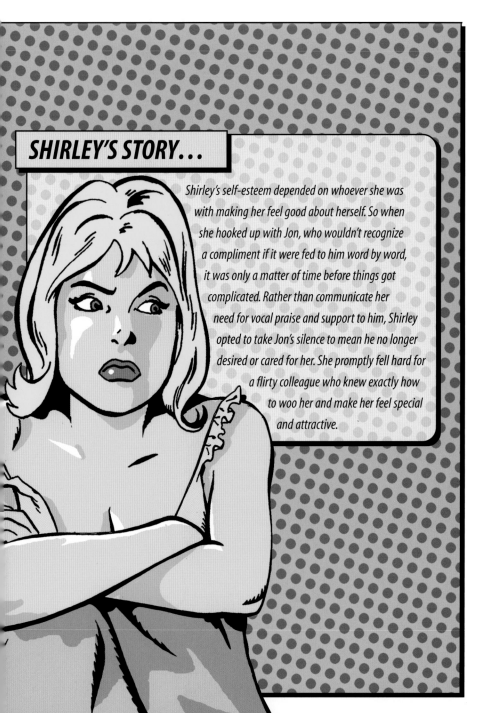

SHIRLEY'S STORY...

Shirley's self-esteem depended on whoever she was with making her feel good about herself. So when she hooked up with Jon, who wouldn't recognize a compliment if it were fed to him word by word, it was only a matter of time before things got complicated. Rather than communicate her need for vocal praise and support to him, Shirley opted to take Jon's silence to mean he no longer desired or cared for her. She promptly fell hard for a flirty colleague who knew exactly how to woo her and make her feel special and attractive.

QUICK FIXES FOR YOUR SELF-ESTEEM

Self-esteem is nothing more than treating yourself the way you treat those you value and care about; it's about being your own best friend. Try these simple measures to boost your self-esteem.

There are dozens of books and courses you can find to help you shore up any areas where you think your self-esteem has gone missing. If your need is urgent, however, and you want something that's going to work a little faster, try out a few of these quick-fix self-esteem boosters.

CHERISH YOURSELF...

1 Keep a diary or notebook in your bag and jot down every positive thing anyone says about you: about your work, the way you look, something you've said or done, about what you mean to them. At the start and end of each day read through the comments—and take a minute or two to concentrate on them and to believe in them.

2 In the same book write down a list of all the great people in your life, both now and in your past. Take a look at each of them and think about what makes them special. Then ask yourself why, if you're such a loser, would so many terrific people choose to spend time with you? Because you're great too, that's why.

3 Treat yourself in the same way that you would treat something precious. Long baths with wonderful moisturizer, regular hair appointments, one or two beautifully fitting outfits that scream class rather than a closet full of "they'll do's." If a guy treated you that way you'd feel cherished. Self-esteem is about cherishing yourself.

4 Learn not to be hard on yourself. How do you react when a friend's feeling down? Next time you're down on yourself for any reason try and take a step back and talk to yourself the way you would someone else. Forgive your "friend," cuddle her, support her, pick her up, and let her know you know she's doing her very best and that that's good enough.

QUICK FIXES FOR YOUR SELF-ESTEEM CONTINUED

Since you're back at (management) school, here's something else to try— market yourself! On a piece of paper write down all the positive things about you. Don't stop till you've reached 30 items, no matter how you struggle. If you find yourself flagging, imagine you're describing yourself in positive terms to someone who doesn't know you. Do a real sales job on yourself: don't stop until you have the interest of a large imaginary audience. Opposite you'll find a few prompts to help you. When you're done take a look at your list: that's the amazing package on offer to some very lucky guy.

THINK POSITIVE!

Struggling to reach three, never mind thirty?
Think about what the answers to these questions say about you:

1 Why do your friends like being with you?

2 What have you done that's made your family proud of you?

3 What's the bravest thing you've ever done?

4 Are there times when you make people laugh?

5 What are the qualities that got you into your current job?

6 What's the best feature on your face?

7 And what do you like best about your body?

8 What excites you?

9 Do you have any hobbies or interests?

10 Think of a time when you overcame the odds—what qualities helped you do that?

11 What about the things in your life you do for others—what do they say about you?

12 How would your best friend describe you?

IT TAKES TWO

Self-esteem cuts both ways. Of course, it's important for yours to be high, but if you've accomplished this at the expense of your partner's feelings, you're headed for trouble. Healthy relationships are about high self-esteem all around.

Healthy self-esteem is at the heart of every strong relationship. But that cuts both ways—you need your guy's self-esteem to be just as high as yours.

Otherwise he'll interpret every suggestion you make as criticism, and every request as a signal he's failed to please you.

LARRY AND EVA'S STORY...

Larry and Eva's rose-tinted glasses came off (along with the gloves) very soon after they first got together.

Things were fine while they were just seeing each other—especially as Eva's friends kept telling her how good-looking Larry was and how lucky she was to have him. But once Larry moved in, Eva realized that her guy's good looks were largely the result of daily two-hour grooming sessions in their bathroom.

She began by poking fun at him, grumbling each time she couldn't get in to fetch what she wanted. Then, on a particularly fraught morning, when she really had to be out of the house early, Eva started yelling at Larry. She accused him of being vain, self-obsessed, and selfish—and of loving to look at himself more than he liked looking at her.

On the other side of the door Larry felt first foolish, then angry, and finally hurt because he knew the way he looked was important to Eva. She'd told him often enough how she liked the fact that all her friends envied his great looks.

IT TAKES TWO CONTINUED

According to the experts, we humans have selective hearing. When people praise us, we hear a whisper. When they criticize us, we hear a shout. It takes dozens of positive messages to counter the effect of one negative one (just ask any parent).

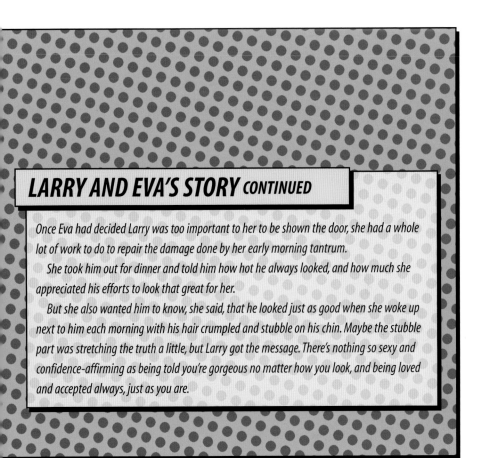

LARRY AND EVA'S STORY CONTINUED

Once Eva had decided Larry was too important to her to be shown the door, she had a whole lot of work to do to repair the damage done by her early morning tantrum.

She took him out for dinner and told him how hot he always looked, and how much she appreciated his efforts to look that great for her.

But she also wanted him to know, she said, that he looked just as good when she woke up next to him each morning with his hair crumpled and stubble on his chin. Maybe the stubble part was stretching the truth a little, but Larry got the message. There's nothing so sexy and confidence-affirming as being told you're gorgeous no matter how you look, and being loved and accepted always, just as you are.

At the school of man management this is the most important lesson of all. You'll progress further and faster if your "training program" for him feels positive. Pay attention to his self-esteem as well as to your own and, when you can, find things to praise rather than fail him on. Don't act cynically, because it'll help you to get your way (he'll see through that right away) but because you love him, or could love him and know that, usually, he's trying hard to get it right. Just think about the glow you get when you get it right: when the gift you've chosen makes someone's eyes light up, or a few carefully chosen words transform a friend's mood. We love getting it right for those we care about. The happier he thinks he's making you, the happier he'll be.

YOU SEXY

THING

UNLIKE YOUR MOM'S GENERATION, THE CHANCES ARE THAT TODAY YOU'LL GET TO KNOW YOUR GUY'S BODY LONG BEFORE YOU EVEN KNOW HIS SHIRT SIZE, MUCH LESS HIS VIEWS ON LOVE AND COMMITMENT. THE CATCH IS THAT IF YOU FAIL TO GET ON IN BED YOU MAY NEVER GET ANY FURTHER. YOU'LL WRITE HIM OFF AS A LOSER RATHER THAN A LOVER. WHICH IS WHY IT'S IMPORTANT THAT YOU GET THE SEX LIFE YOU WANT. THE SAME IS TRUE IF YOU AND HE ARE ALREADY AN ITEM, BUT YOUR SEX LIFE HAS NEVER MADE THE BED SHAKE, MUCH LESS THE EARTH MOVE. WHEN YOU FIRST GOT TOGETHER YOU WERE SO KEEN YOU CLOSED YOUR EYES TO HIS LESS-THAN-OVERWHELMING PERFORMANCE. NOW YOU'VE DECIDED HE MAY BE A KEEPER, HOW WILL YOU BREAK THE NEWS THAT YOUR FUTURE DEPENDS ON HIM DELIVERING?

PERFECT MATCH?

The secret of great sex is recognizing that you and your guy are different in terms of what you want and need from your sexual relationship. For the best sex use your knowledge of these differences to foster a sex life that leaves you both feeling great—and satisfied.

Ali's story demonstrates that we could all do with a Sam in our life. The truth is that when it comes to lovemaking, no-one will understand what you're talking about as well as another girl. Just watch your friends nodding in sympathy and recognition when you complain about the way your guy touches you as if he was tuning a radio, or interprets a peck on the cheek as an overt invitation to full-blown sex.

The physical differences between men and women aren't only about who's taller, stronger, or faster, but about what goes on in bed. He experiences sex differently and thinks about it differently from you.

If you want your sex life to run as sweetly as Ali and Sam's then understanding where he's coming from will help you get what you want—and see he does too.

ALI'S STORY...

Up to the time Ali met Sam she'd thought of sex as an optional extra. If it went OK it was a bonus, but finding a good lover was nowhere near as important to her as having someone to go out with, to take to parties, and to talk to late at night when she was stressed from work. Post-Sam Ali could talk of nothing else. She hadn't known sex could be this good. Sam understood her body brilliantly, knew just where and how to touch, and had shown her lots of things she'd never even considered (and which her friends didn't ask her to go into—too much information!). Sam even understood when Ali only wanted a cuddle; she got her hugs without it turning into a battle about whether or not they were going to have sex.

...OR MISMATCH?

With apologies to all those guys out there who understand us perfectly, know exactly what we like and how we like it...for the other 99 percent, there are four main areas where the gap between the sexes is a major trip hazard.

1 TOUCH

There's good and bad news here. The good news is that in the right hands your whole body is an erogenous zone. Once you're in the mood he can turn you on just by joining the dots on your freckles. The bad news is that 90 percent of what he's about is focused between his legs. So though he's heard that girls like foreplay, he doesn't really understand it and can't wait for the moment when you give him the green light for penetration.

This also explains why he thinks it's OK to touch you heavy handedly. You need to understand that his nerve endings are buried: how else could guys survive a game of football? You need to demonstrate to him that you're a sensitive flower who only needs a light touch to be brought to boiling point.

By the same token, you need to ask him how he likes to be touched. Your subtle handling may just feel irritating to him, and he may want something much bolder.

2 DESIRE

Estimates vary about how often guys think about sex, from once an hour to once every three minutes. There are times when you suddenly think about sex too, like when the guy from IT with the nice butt is fiddling with your hard drive. But for the most part, you probably find that it enters your thoughts only when you're feeling close to the guy in your life. It's well established that girls tend to come at sex through our feelings.

He, on the other hand, can think about sex quite removed from any emotions, attachment, or intimacy. You're far more likely to hear him talk about his feelings after sex, as if the physical release of sex has unlocked the secret door, behind which he hides his emotions.

What does this mean for your sex life? That he doesn't understand he needs to show his feelings for you to get you in the mood. Or that the route into your underwear is through your ears, making sure—with the help of wine, roses, and romance—that you feel loved up. Whereas he's raring to go the moment you touch him (probably before!). It's a classic Mars and Venus divide: most girls can't do sex from a standing start. Teach him he has to warm your engine first.

47

...OR MISMATCH? CONTINUED

3 SEX EDUCATION

We're not talking school biology books, but about what you and he have learned about sex on your way to getting together. While you've been willing to wade through 760 pages of a novel before reaching its climax (literally)—the moment where the hero and heroine make passionate love—his literary influences are more likely to have been magazines. The type in which the full-on pictures do have captions, but in which the words are hardly the point. And while you were laughing and crying over chick flicks he and his mates were lusting over porn. Girls and guys grow up surrounded by influences that further distance our already very different attitudes to sex.

Time for an adult education class: share with him the pictures, the films and TV, sights, tastes, art and music, and sensations that you find erotic. He will soon work out that if he pays attention he'll be able to do excellent practical work—and win your top marks.

4 GOAL

For some reason men are programmed to be much more about the end rather than the means; they're orgasm-oriented. Whereas sometimes girls do just want to have fun, or cuddles, or massage, or some other kind of contact that doesn't necessary have to lead to full-blown lovemaking. You're going to have to convince him it's possible to enjoy the journey as much as the destination—use some of the tips on pp. 53–55 to ensure that your sex life is satisfying you both.

Whether you use words, moves, gestures, or exciting noises, it's all about communicating. After all, the poor guy needs someone to take his sex education in hand: all the time you've been swapping notes with your girlfriends and learning the basics from magazines, the sex talk he's had with his friends is probably solely about when and who with.

A word about timing here. Remember what we said about men getting to their feelings through sex? Well that's the time, when he's melted in your arms, to say how great it was for you, and suggest ways he could make the earth move for both of you even more next time around.

Our sexual performance is an area where we're all a bit sensitive: worrying about how good we are is something girls and guys share. Make sure nothing in what you say and do suggests he's a failure. You could try bringing up the subject of sex when you can use it to tease you both. Out for a meal perhaps, suggest what you'd like him to try when you get home. He'll be too turned on knowing you're thinking about sex to take your comments as criticism.

PILLOW TALK

Letting him know what you want isn't only about what you say but also about how you behave: your reactions and responses to his moves.

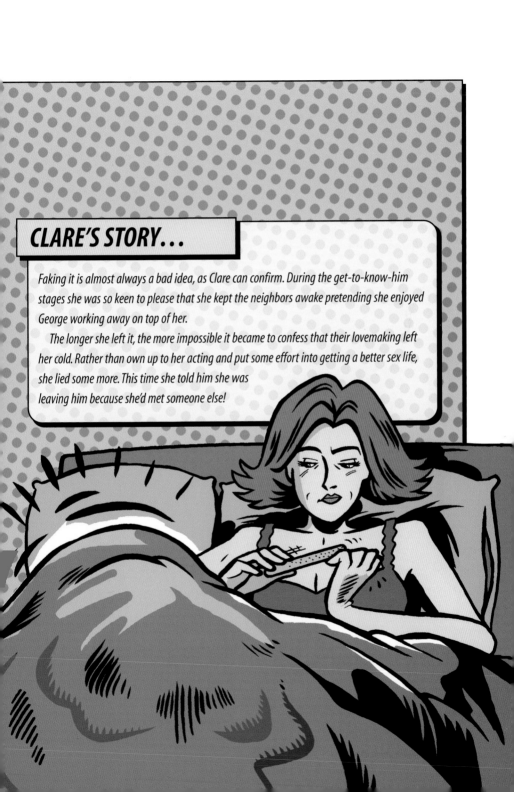

CLARE'S STORY...

Faking it is almost always a bad idea, as Clare can confirm. During the get-to-know-him stages she was so keen to please that she kept the neighbors awake pretending she enjoyed George working away on top of her.

The longer she left it, the more impossible it became to confess that their lovemaking left her cold. Rather than own up to her acting and put some effort into getting a better sex life, she lied some more. This time she told him she was leaving him because she'd met someone else!

TEACH HIM TO TURN YOU ON

They say 70 percent of our communication is wordless, so try putting some of these techniques on the curriculum to let him know what you want without reading him a lecture on your needs.

TURN-ONS YOU'LL BOTH ENJOY...

1 Introduce him to your personal film studies class. Ask him which films he finds erotic, and tell him which ones you find sexy. Then as you watch one of his choices, ask him to tell you why it's such a turn-on. Do the same as you watch your sexy movie— tell him exactly why you find a scene or performance so erotic.

2 Suggest you both sign up for a class in massage. Homework should be fun for you both but, more importantly, he won't feel threatened if he's finding out from other girls that gently, slowly does it.

3 In every survey girls say they want more foreplay (in case you wondered, men say they want more variety). Make foreplay less of a chore for him by stressing the "play:" dress up, get some toys, act out your favorite scenes.

TEACH HIM TO TURN YOU ON CONTINUED

TURN-ONS YOU'LL BOTH ENJOY CONTINUED

4 Show him the ropes. We're not talking S&M here, but the touches that make your body quiver with pleasure. You can turn it into a game by making him sit on a chair fully clothed while you show him exactly where you like to be touched. He'll be so certain he's died and gone to heaven it won't occur to him he's getting a lesson, too.

5 A variation on number 4, above, is to suggest that you both wear blindfolds so you can only use your hands to guide each other to what you want.

6 Sometimes it's hard to concentrate on getting pleasure when you're busy giving it. The answer is to take turns. Allow him to be entirely selfish while he reaches his own orgasm, then he'll be able to give you the attention you deserve.

7 Try sex by the book. On pp. 56-57 are some girls' sex secrets. All you have to do is leave the page open somewhere he's bound to find it.

8 Write him a list of what works for you and hand it to him, together with an invitation to join you for a hotel weekend where he can try it out. Invite him to come up with his own list and to take you somewhere for a bit of study time.

9 Together beg, borrow, or buy a sex manual, then take it in turns to choose which of the delights within you're going to experiment with. There's no rule to say you can't choose a particular technique or position over and over again. He'd have to be dense not to get the message.

10 Have fun with make-believe. Both of you get to choose your favorite turn-on scene from the movies, then it's lights down and action, as you act it out. However dubious your acting, you'll still win the award for turning in a great performance.

YOU AND HE HAVE GROWN UP LEARNING ABOUT LOVE AND SEX FROM VERY DIFFERENT SOURCES—WHICH CAN LEAD TO WIDELY DIFFERING EXPECTATIONS.

Get him to understand how you work and he'll always get it right.

SEXY SECRETS TO SHARE WITH YOUR GUY

WHAT TO SHOW AND TELL HIM

1 *The tongue is as mighty as the tool, and no, we're not talking oral sex, but how turned on we get when a guy takes the time to tell us we're gorgeous and can't keep his hands off us. Making us feel attractive is a massive turn-on as long as it's genuine.*

2 *Foreplay is anything that helps us relax and leave the rest of our lives behind. So long before the first kiss, he could try running you a bath with scented oils, massaging your shoulders, or sitting you down in front of the fire with a glass of wine while he does any chores around the house. What a turn-on!*

3 *Since we need to relax we hate guys who make us feel we're taking too long to get turned on. Never let us feel that you're checking on us.*

4 Lots of girls fantasize about being seduced. We've never quite given up on romantic fiction which is why we go weak-kneed when Rhett sweeps Scarlett into his arms and takes her to bed. He should try it!

5 Slowly does it. By and large it takes longer for us to be aroused. Instead of starting in bed, he could slowly take your clothes off and watch you melt (or just watch you— if his eyes are telling you they love what they're seeing and his hands are turning you on big time, you'll melt even more).

6 Our equipment is different, and the things that feel good to him—hard massage, strong moves—may have us climbing the walls. And not in the right way.

7 When we're turned on it feels good to be touched everywhere, so instead of homing straight in on what's inside our underwear he could try making love to our arms, ankles, back of our neck, ears, toes. OK, we give in!

8 Try something that doesn't usually have sexual overtones. Read to us, or put on a piece of music to soften and warm the mood before you make any sexual moves.

9 Girls are big on mood and setting. If the room's a mess and the sheets are still crumpled from last night, it's unlikely we'll ever get past first base.

10 At the end of a lousy day, lovemaking can feel too much like hard labor. But we're always in the mood for a foot or back massage . . . and who knows where that might lead?

It is no real secret that knowing he's turning you on is a turn-on: guys are scared of not being good enough. Yes, some of them talk as if they're the world's greatest lover but, deep down, men are worried about failing to live up (or get up) to your expectations.

You've probably heard the joke that says all a woman needs to do to be a good lover is to show up. Of course it's not true—but it does reveal how much the guys still feel the onus is on them to deliver the goods.

That's why, while helping him to learn about your body, it's a mistake to criticize or compare. Men can't help but compete against each other all the time, and they're rarely honest enough with their friends to find out that in fact they all share the same fears and doubts. If you give him the impression your last lover was better than him, you'll have to be prepared for a vanishing act.

That may mean you have to be economical with the truth, even to the extent of not letting on quite what an expert you are (if, indeed, that's happens to be the case). He'll think the more experience you've had, the more potential for him to fail to match up to your former lovers.

Let him know you think he's a sex god, though, and he'll continue to put in the effort to ensure he takes you to paradise…at which point you'll realize that, thanks to all your help, he really has become one!

PARADISE IS TWICE AS NICE

Because he is goal-centered, the biggest turn-on your guy can have is to see and feel that he is turning you on.

KIRSTY'S STORY...

The first few times Kirsty went back to Jim's place for a sexy session were thrillingly exciting. She'd never had sex like this, with a guy who was really fit and proud of it. But it didn't take all that long for ecstasy to turn into exhaustion as she tried unsuccessfully to keep up with her athletic partner. After one particularly long and tortuous bout of floor, beam, and upside-down exercises Kirsty decided Jim really ought to have been called "Gym." And since she'd never enjoyed phys. ed. at school (and had no intention of joining the gym) it was time to quit his classes.

Healthy relationships are those where both partners get what they want. So use what you've learned about his sexual make-up to take him to paradise too. In business, they call it incentivizing, but we'll just call it great lovemaking.

HOW TO HAVE HIM EATING FROM YOUR HAND

GIVING AS GOOD AS YOU GET...

1 Most men love to receive oral sex. If you enjoy it, learn how to give it to him for the kind of sex that really can go anywhere, any time.

2 Surprise him: remember what the guys said about loving variety? If you always do it in bed it's bound to become repetitive. Take him out of the house and get up close and personal to a tree/sand dune/car hood/somewhere where the danger of being caught adds an extra edge to your encounter.

3 Let him know how sexy you find him. Just like you, he wants to be wanted— knowing you want him makes him want you even more.

4 This one is a bit of a cliché but in surveys guys say they love to watch themselves making out. It's time to polish and position that mirror. Sometimes clichés work.

5 Have an orgasm. Remember, he's goal-oriented, so making you come is like a home run and the winning goal rolled into one!

6 Offer him a quickie sometimes. You may not be in the mood but it's a lovely way to show him you're also aware of his sexual needs, and fast, furious sex can be a turn-on when you see how much he wants you.

7 Give him a wake-up call with a difference. It's a shame to waste that hard-on every morning. Starting the day with a big "O" beats starting the day with a big breakfast hands down.

LEAN ON

ME

INDEPENDENCE IS ONE THING, GOING IT ALONE IS ANOTHER. NO MATTER HOW CONFIDENT YOU ARE, OR HOW WELL YOU STAND ON YOUR OWN TWO FEET, EVERYONE NEEDS SOMEONE TO SMOOTH THEIR WAY THROUGH LIFE'S UPS AND DOWNS, TO OFFER PRACTICAL AND EMOTIONAL SUPPORT, AND SOMETIMES JUST TO BE ON THEIR SIDE. THE TROUBLE IS "SUPPORT" MEANS DIFFERENT THINGS TO DIFFERENT PEOPLE. LIKE WHEN YOU WANT SUPPORT AND HE GIVES YOU "HELPFUL" CRITICISM, OR YOU ASK HIM TO BE THERE FOR YOU, AND ALL OF A SUDDEN HE'S THERE ALL THE TIME, WHETHER YOU WANT IT OR NOT. WHETHER YOU'RE AFTER A QUICK HUG FOR LUCK OR A MAJOR THERAPY SESSION, UNDERSTANDING HOW HE TICKS IS THE MOST EFFECTIVE WAY TO ENSURE THAT YOU'LL GET WHAT YOU NEED FROM YOUR GUY EVERY TIME.

A WORLD OF DIFFERENCE

Once upon a time, all a guy had to do was to bring home a bear so we wouldn't go hungry. Times have changed, but men are still hard-wired in the same way.

These days women can buy their food from the store, and earn the money to pay for it. What we want from the men in our life has got more complicated: love, affection, approval, support, understanding, humor, fun—and the sensitivity to know which of those we want and when.

It's a tall order for anyone, but especially for someone whose make-up, beneath the surface, is still largely shaped by his bear-stalking history.

Many of the things that stand in the way of you getting what you want stem from the fact that their roles in the world meant that guys and girls developed differently.

So you've got two choices: grin and bear the fact that he never knows when to give you a hug, never remembers your anniversary, and always seems to say the wrong thing—if he says anything at all.

Or you take those differences as your starting point so that you can get what you want by playing to his strengths, rather than setting him up to fail and paving the way for you to feel let down.

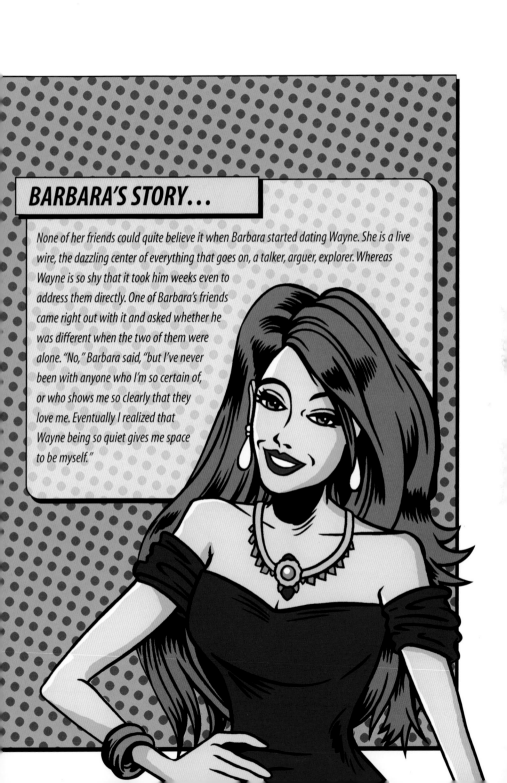

BARBARA'S STORY...

None of her friends could quite believe it when Barbara started dating Wayne. She is a live
wire, the dazzling center of everything that goes on, a talker, arguer, explorer. Whereas
Wayne is so shy that it took him weeks even to
address them directly. One of Barbara's friends
came right out with it and asked whether he
was different when the two of them were
alone. "No," Barbara said, "but I've never
been with anyone who I'm so certain of,
or who shows me so clearly that they
love me. Eventually I realized that
Wayne being so quiet gives me space
to be myself."

Understanding some of the fundamental differences in the ways girls and guys think can go a long way toward avoiding misunderstandings.

LITTLE THINGS PLEASE

MARIA'S STORY...

In the six years she was with Dominic, Maria hated the way he missed every important date in her calendar. She was the one who remembered to send birthday gifts to their friends, to check on sick relatives, and to book a table at their favorite restaurant when their anniversary came around.

Each time it happened they fought more bitterly because, as far as Maria was concerned, Dominic's inability to remember red-letter days meant they didn't matter to him. If he loved her, he'd realize that they were important to her and get his act together.

On the other side, Dominic felt that, knowing he was bad at remembering day-to-day events, Maria was laying traps for him: instead of reminding him of key dates, she was biding her time, ready to pounce when he failed to spot them.

Sadly, there are millions of Dominics and Marias, getting angry with each other every day. Because most guys aren't big on detail—and most girls are.

That's how come he'll sling on the first tie his fingers touch when he looks in the closet, even though fluorescent orange stripes against his green shirt make him look like a candy bar. You, on the other hand, having slipped into a tailored suit, spend hours choosing a bag, shoes, and earrings to match.

While he was stalking wild animals for supper that was all he had to think about. Whereas you were gathering firewood, looking after the children and domestic animals, collecting foods in case he came home empty handed, and handling all the other "small stuff" that makes life run smoothly for everyone.

LITTLE THINGS PLEASE CONTINUED

PAY ATTENTION...

You need him to pay attention to the small stuff in order for you to feel cherished by him. These are the sort of gestures that make all the difference.

1 Remembering when something important is happening in your life and asking you about it.

2 Sending flowers to your office or buying you small gifts on your anniversary—or just to thank you for being there.

3 Telling you he loves you every day rather than saving it for a once-in-a-blue-moon grand gesture.

4 Noticing when you've cut your hair or you've spent the afternoon rearranging the pictures on the wall, or the books on the bookshelf.

Now that you've thought about what you need, help him to get the important things right for you.

Don't take it personally when he forgets things; he can't help it and, brilliant as you are, you're unlikely to be able to reconfigure his DNA in a single lifetime. Instead, help him to understand your programming and priorities with the following techniques.

BIG STUFF, SMALL STUFF...

1 *Get a big wall calendar, or share your diaries on the computer, and make time once a week to sit down together and write in every important date and appointment.*

2 *Show him the joy of the small stuff: send him flowers from time to time, slip loving or sexy notes into his pocket, e-mail him a poem, or dress up for dinner at home. From the day we're born we learn by example. At the girls' school of man management these are your practical sessions; in time, he'll get the message.*

3 *Tell him what matters to you, don't leave him to guess. If you know you're going to get resentful if he forgets a key date, warn him in advance (in a friendly, not a nagging way) and give him some idea of how excited you are about it, so he doesn't disappoint.*

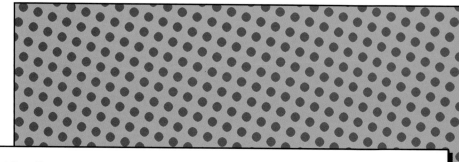

Like all guys, yours is programmed to do one thing or think about one thing at a time—unlike girls, for whom multitasking comes as naturally as breathing.

ONE THING ON HIS MIND

Well, apart from sex that is. Because of their programming men struggle to concentrate on more than one thing at a time. That's why he gets mad if you notice the plants need watering while you're making out.

This is great if you're in bed and getting the benefit of his undivided attention—but it's a recipe for a major stand-off if you've spent hours getting ready to go on a date and he's still fiddling underneath the hood of the car trying to connect two wires and oblivious to the time.

Or you want to talk about the awful day you've just had, and he's watching the game. If all you can get out of him is a grunt, it doesn't mean he loves football more than you. It means that unlike you, he can't talk on the phone, do his nails, and keep an eye on his favorite soap all at the same time.

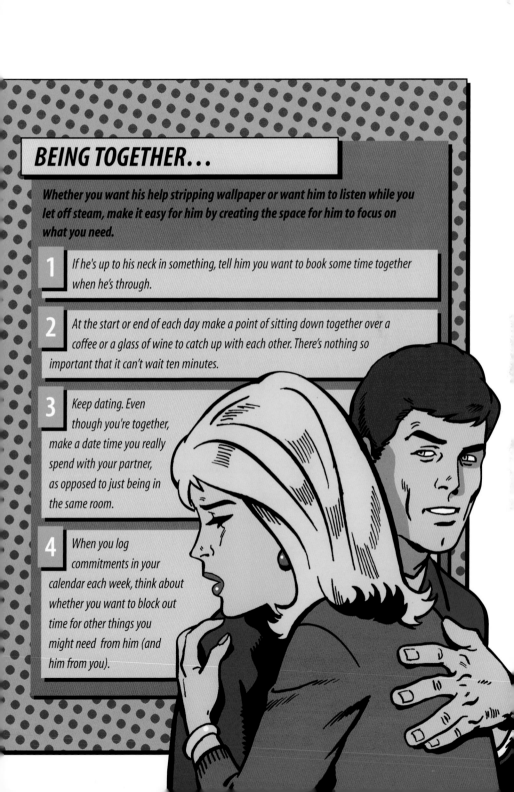

BEING TOGETHER...

Whether you want his help stripping wallpaper or want him to listen while you let off steam, make it easy for him by creating the space for him to focus on what you need.

1 *If he's up to his neck in something, tell him you want to book some time together when he's through.*

2 *At the start or end of each day make a point of sitting down together over a coffee or a glass of wine to catch up with each other. There's nothing so important that it can't wait ten minutes.*

3 *Keep dating. Even though you're together, make a date time you really spend with your partner, as opposed to just being in the same room.*

4 *When you log commitments in your calendar each week, think about whether you want to block out time for other things you might need from him (and him from you).*

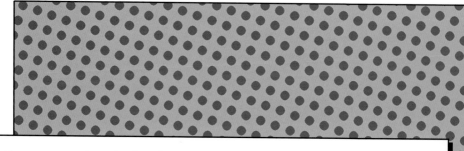

Have you ever thought that the reason that a dog may be a man's best friend is because it never says "We need to talk"?

A LITTLE LESS TALK, A LITTLE MORE ACTION

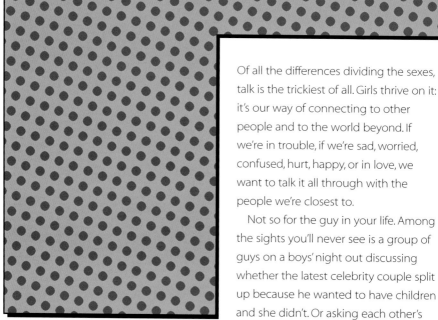

Of all the differences dividing the sexes, talk is the trickiest of all. Girls thrive on it: it's our way of connecting to other people and to the world beyond. If we're in trouble, if we're sad, worried, confused, hurt, happy, or in love, we want to talk it all through with the people we're closest to.

Not so for the guy in your life. Among the sights you'll never see is a group of guys on a boys' night out discussing whether the latest celebrity couple split up because he wanted to have children and she didn't. Or asking each other's

advice on whether now is a good time to move in with their latest girlfriend.

Your guy is programmed for deeds, not words. And he certainly doesn't understand your habit of "thinking aloud." As far as he's concerned, if you say it, you mean it. For this reason, he's likely to take your words at face value, whether you really mean them or not. And he'll want to come up with solutions even when all you want to do is to share a worry: as far as he's concerned, if words don't lead to action then he doesn't see any point in them.

You think talking to each other is about bringing you closer, sharing yourself with him the way you do with your girlfriends. Whereas inside his head the alarm bell is going off in case he says the wrong thing—or at least the wrong thing at this moment—or you tie him in knots. After all, in a normal day you get twice as much practice at using words as he does; it is estimated that the average woman will speak around 23,000 words, compared with the average man's total of half that amount, a mere 12,000.

A LITTLE LESS TALK, A LITTLE MORE ACTION
CONTINUED

If talking and listening is what you want, make it as unthreatening as you can. Get into the habit of getting him talking without announcing that that's what you're doing: over dinner perhaps, or while you're out on a walk, so he starts to associate talking with having a great time with you.

There will be times when you need him to listen or open up because of something that's going on in your life. Get the ball rolling by asking for his advice on something else: remember, he's more comfortable in problem-solving mode and once you're talking you've got his attention. Or satisfy his desire for action by suggesting he massages your shoulders or gives you a cuddle while you unload to him.

Of course not all communication involves talking. All that time working alongside the other girls in the cave has made you an expert in intuitively sharing in what people are thinking or feeling. You instinctively know when a friend is feeling down, just as you know the right thing to say or do to support her when she's feeling low or is grappling with a problem. Your guy, however, almost certainly lacks this sixth sense.

It's vital you're aware of this glaring gap in his communications toolkit if you're to get the practical and emotional support you want. He can't read your mind—back rub, cuddle, a long romantic session, or even just a compliment on what you're wearing: if you want something from him you are going to have to tell him, in a clear, straightforward way. And almost certainly more than once.

ROSE'S STORY...

Rose and Zach were on the point of splitting up when it dawned on Rose that what had changed was they'd stopped paying attention to one another. When they were dating, their time together was about listening and sharing and having fun. Once they moved in together their conversations were about practical stuff. And sharing meant sitting on the sofa gazing at the TV rather than each other. The TV "off" switch and some talk therapy helped them to recover their mutual sense of what the other was thinking, feeling, and wanting.

A GIRL'S GUIDE TO ASKING FOR WHAT YOU WANT

He can't guess what you want and need—you're going to have to tell him. These pointers will allow you to do that, with success.

Your intuition means you are almost sure to pick up on the second "meaning" behind your friends' words. But it can be a mistake to read more into anything he is saying. Guys are literal—nine times out of ten he means exactly what he's saying, and no more than that.

That's just one example of the many ways in which girls and guys end up misunderstanding each other. When it comes to you getting what you want, take a leaf from his book and ask him clearly and honestly, using the rules on the next page—you stand a far greater chance of success.

RECIPE FOR SUCCESS

1 Be clear. His one-track mind can't cope with hints so there's no point hedging around what you're after. "I'm feeling so exhausted. Will you tidy up tonight?" is a perfectly reasonable request and likely to get better results than an hour's worth of deep sighing about how much you have to do before you can crash.

2 Be positive. If you possibly can, focus on what you do want rather than what you don't, and on his strengths rather than his weaknesses. Maybe he's incapable of recognizing when you just need a comforting cuddle. But once you've told him that you need one, you may find that he gives the best hugs.

3 Be timely. It's not a good idea to try to tackle big topics when you're feeling out of sorts with him, or with yourself. Whoever recommended not going to sleep on an argument clearly didn't understand the power of sleep to smooth some of the rough edges and bring a bit of perspective to problems which seem huge in the middle of the night. It's also easier to find a solution when you are both calm.

4 Be fair. We all love to give but sometimes it's good to get. Remember, he hasn't had the benefit of reading this book so as you become more expert in wrapping him around your finger, don't forget that he's got needs too!

5 Be honest. Women don't always find it easy to be assertive. Instead we take the long way around trying to justify what we're asking for. You don't need to justify any more than you need to explain beyond the simple truth that when you ask for something it's because it will make you happy. When we care about someone we like to make them happy—there's nothing wrong with that.

Make getting what you want a game that you both play and enjoy—with the added pay-off that you'll learn a lot about each other.

PLAY THE GAME

Even the best relationships can rapidly fall into a rut. One day you realize that you really should have been honest about what you like and dislike sooner. Don't walk into this trap: you can have a lot of fun teaching each other what you want, without anyone feeling they're under attack for having failed to deliver. The wishlist game gives you a chance to tell each other exactly what you mean by practical and emotional support: the things that will win the highest marks for both of you.

HAPPY BIRTHDAY

Next time his birthday or yours comes around, suggest you give each other a different kind of gift. Take a piece of

paper each and on it write down a list of the things you want from each other. They need to be practical: obviously you want his love but what is it you want him to do to show you he loves you?

Agree a number limit, somewhere between 10 and 20, so that each is a small thing in itself, but they add up to a huge difference in how you feel. Then, stick the lists where you can both check in with them and make a note every time your partner does something on the list. At the end of a week, add the points up and agree a prize for the one who's scored the most hits: an evening of luxury being waited on hand and foot, perhaps?

WHAT I REALLY WANT IS...

Below, you'll see a few ideas to get you started. "Her" list is in the left-hand column, and his is in the right-hand one. Remember this is supposed to be fun; it's not there as payback time, or a chance for one of you to turn round and say "you never do anything for me."

You to bring me breakfast in bed	You to let me have the sports section
You to tell me you love me	You to tell me you love me
A hug	A sex session initiated by you
You to notice what I'm wearing	You to give me time out when I get home
You to look at me when we make love	You to wear sexy lingerie
You to remember my friends' names	To go out with my friends guilt-free

GUYS KNOW THAT TALKING ISN'T THEIR STRONG SUIT, SO PLAY GAMES THAT WILL REDUCE THEIR RELUCTANCE TO RISK IT, AND TO ENCOURAGE THEM TO TALK ABOUT WHAT'S ON THEIR MIND.

HIGH MAINTENANCE, RICH REWARDS

Relationships work when the two people involved accept that the love, friendship, and support they get out is more than worth the effort that they put in.

Guys like to pretend among themselves that we want too much from them. That's why they buy handcuffs for stag nights and joke about life sentences.

Lean on some of them too hard and they'll collapse like an underdone pavlova, leaving a squidgy mess where you thought there was a man.

(It can work the other way of course. If you believe he's too needy, you may decide you'd rather save your energy for someone who isn't with you because he thinks you can fix his life for him.)

Using the techniques we've covered should save you from a disaster, leaving him in no doubt that if you've got a future together it'll be because you're both getting what you want. You're grown-up enough to know that you're two individuals, but also to recognize that you can be even more together— the best you can be—in a healthy, loving relationship.

Any relationship worth having is high maintenance, but when you get it right the rewards are immense.

LISA'S STORY...

One of things that drew Joe to Lisa was her sense of adventure. Yet he quickly grew to resent the weekends she headed off with her rock climbing friends. Joe said if Lisa loved him she wouldn't want to spend so much time away from him, or put him through the worry of waiting for her safe return. Though Lisa briefly hung up her mountaineering gear, eventually she started to see that loving is not the same as smothering. In the end, their relationship became the casualty.

MANAGING

HIS MONEY

YOU'VE HAD A FANTASTIC EVENING, DINING OUT ON LOBSTER AND CHAMPAGNE, AND NOW THE VIBES BETWEEN YOU ARE SO HIGHLY CHARGED THAT YOU'VE GOT A GREAT DEAL MORE THAN CHEESECAKE IN MIND FOR DESSERT. THEN YOUR DATE CALLS FOR THE CHECK AND YOU FEEL A SHIVER OF ANXIETY. YOU'RE NOT WORRYING ABOUT WHEN YOU MAKE IT INTO THE BEDROOM. WHAT'S ON YOUR MIND IS MONEY: IS HE EXPECTING YOU TO PAY YOUR WAY, OR WILL HE BE INSULTED IF YOU OFFER? CAN YOU AFFORD TO GO DUTCH? OR, AS YOU ASKED HIM OUT, WILL HE ASSUME YOU'RE PICKING UP THE WHOLE TAB?

IN AN AGE WHERE THERE IS ALMOST NO TOPIC OFF-LIMITS FOR DISCUSSION WITH FRIENDS AND COLLEAGUES, MONEY REMAINS THE GREAT TABOO—WHICH IS GOING TO MAKE IT THAT MUCH HARDER FOR YOU TO HELP HIM TO MANAGE HIS FINANCIAL AFFAIRS.

Some girls find the money taboo works brilliantly in their favor, as demonstrated by Kay's story, opposite. But the truth is that from the day they got together Kay assumed she had as much right to spend Simon's money as her own. If they were going to be sharing a home, a bed, and a future, they should certainly be sharing money too. Not to pool his resources would be like saying money was more important than love, commitment, and trust—in other words the things that are really the most important in relationships.

Perhaps no child-free couple really needs a full set of clean towels for every day of the week, six varieties of scented candle in each room, and more original art on the walls than any downtown gallery. But shopping makes Kay happy, and if she's happy, Simon's happy too. He loves coming home to his excited wife, bursting to share her pleasure in "their" latest purchases with him. Excitement, pleasure, and approval work better than aphrodisiacs where love's concerned, so his homecoming is always special for them both.

Kay's never considered complaining about Simon's absences because as far as she's concerned her life is a perfect mix of man and Mammon, sex and shopping. And the more content she is, the more her feelings spread to Simon and the more goodwill there is to go around in the relationship.

HIS MONEY AND HER LOVE

You may know everything there is to know about your guy—but still feel unable to ask the million-dollar questions about money.

KAY'S STORY...

Kay's partner Simon is keeping her in fabulous style—and he gets no say in the matter. He earns it, she spends it. Simple as that. Simon works for three out of every four weeks on an oil field where there's nothing to buy. Kay's argument is that going out and spending lavishly on homewares and antiques is her way of compensating for his absence, and making sure he's got a palace to come back to. She would say that the money is theirs, and she doesn't spend it on herself, simply on making life more comfortable for both of them.

MONEY MATTERS

Instead of feeling that money's controlling you, you need to control it. To do this, you need to understand your own attitudes to money, and where they come from.

Before we go any further let's just be clear that, for most of us, Simon is as rare a creature as a million-dollar bill. It's (relatively) easy to be relaxed about sharing your money when you've got so much of the stuff that a convoy of Chanel No. 5 wouldn't register as a blip on your bank manager's radar. If you do meet a multi-millionaire, be like Kay and kiss your gift horse straight on the mouth rather than staring into it.

For the vast majority of us, our relationship with money is as tricky as our relationships with people. We worry we have too little (even when we have enough), fear that instead of controlling it, it's controlling us, and we hate having to think about it.

AND WHAT ABOUT YOU?

1 Are you the kind of girl who loves feeling financially independent and always wants to pay her way?

2 Do you do so out of fairness or card-carrying-feminist principle; or do you do so reluctantly, even when you can't afford it, in case he thinks you're a freeloader, or that he can buy you?

3 Are you a Kay, happy that what's his is yours (and what's yours is yours too), entirely comfortable letting him pick up most of the bills because he earns more than you do?

4 Are you simply doing things the way they were always done in your home? Or do you think he should pay because you believe the many things you contribute to the relationship more than balance the books?

What you and your guy feel about money will almost certainly depend on how much of it you have, how much your families had, their attitudes to it, plus all the ups and downs you've had with money along the way.

Before you tackle money matters with him, try to get a handle on where you're coming from.

Challenge yourself with some of these common girl hang-ups to see whether your attitudes could be getting in the way of making your relationship healthy, wealthy, and honest.

GIRLS AND MONEY

DO YOU, OR DON'T YOU?

1 *Do you ever lie to people about how much something cost? Do you even lie to yourself about how much you have actually spent?*

2 *If so, what's the reason: embarrassment, guilt, or sensitivity because you know they haven't got much money?*

3 *Have you ever hidden bank or credit card statements from your nearest and dearest? If so, why?*

4 *Do you shove your bank statements into a drawer without checking them in case it's bad news?*

5 Do you sometimes go shopping even when you know you're flat broke—and still come back with loads of carrier bags?

6 Do you feel you have to make excuses if you don't buy the cheapest brand of any product you need?

7 Think back to your other boyfriends: how much did you know about their salary, bank balance, and financial track record? (And before you say "plenty" compare it with what you knew about their ex-girlfriends/favorite meal/shoe size.)

8 Have you ever shared that information with any of the guys in your life? How about the current one?

If any of these questions makes you feel uncomfortable about money, you're in good company. We girls have only had our own bank accounts for a couple of generations (and our credit cards for less than that!).

Not only have we got some catching up to do, we've also got a whole lot of guilt to shake off. The chances are your great-grandmother had to ask her husband for every cent she wanted to spend, so she never felt comfortable spending it on herself.

The other thing that can make us feel guilty about spending money is shaky self-esteem. You'd love those slinky black boots but that means treating yourself. Since you don't really believe you're worth it, the minute you splash out, you feel more guilt.

GUYS AND MONEY

It's not easy to generalize about guys' attitudes to what they keep in their back pocket, since they can be as confused as us. But we do all live in a world where what a person earns often seems to count for more than who they are.

The workplace's way of showing someone's doing a great job is to offer more money. His friends will measure his feelings for you by the size of the rock on your finger rather than what he wrote on the card accompanying it.

And though the other guests at a party may be too polite to come right out and ask "what do you earn?" you can bet your bottom dollar they'll have noticed any telltale labels on your clothing or shoes, or checked out the car that you drive.

With their single-minded approach to life, guys tend to buy into this "wealth equals worth" philosophy more than girls. Put simply, the price tag is his way of assessing its value.

Even if he's not fooled by price tags, his attitudes may be shaped by the past. What he's inherited from his ancestors is the need to compete for resources. When it really was a case of survival of the fittest, he needed an edge over other males. Ever since he was an adolescent comparing "lunchboxes" in the locker room he's wanted to be bigger, brighter, faster—and richer—than the next guy.

Our different attitudes to money, aggravated by society's taboo on money talk, are a recipe for misunderstanding. You see money as a way to prove you are worth something, so if he keeps his credit cards padlocked while he's around you, you'll end up thinking he doesn't agree.

Whereas your desire to help relieve him of any surplus cash is undermining his attempts to accumulate more than the next guy (and the guy next to him).

GUYS' ATTITUDE TO HARD CASH IS USUALLY EASY TO FATHOM. IF YOU'VE GOT IT, YOU'RE DOING WELL. IF YOU'VE NOT GOT MUCH, YOU'RE DOING SOMETHING WRONG.

BALANCING THE BOOKS

Love, commitment, and trust may be the foundation stones of a good relationship, but it's money that most couples argue about—and it's money that is more likely than anything else to cause a relationship to break down.

It may not seem romantic, but being honest about money from the outset should prevent some of these misunderstandings and ensure the devil's never in the dollar.

You certainly don't want misplaced guilt getting in the way of reaching sensible arrangements that you're both happy with, any more than you want dishonesty and distrust to turn the control of your resources into a power game between you.

According to a leading relationship counselling charity, some 70 percent of couples argue about money: that's more than about any other topic. So forget investing money, instead invest some time and energy in helping him understand where you're coming from when it comes to money, and on opening the account on his attitudes. That way there's a good chance you'll find a financial set-up that works just fine for you both.

If your guy is earning a great deal more than you it's only fair he pays the bigger portion. Just as, if it's you earning the six figures, you might want to share some of the spoils with him.

You may, on the other hand, agree to hang on to your own respective purse strings and simply operate a straight 50/50 split on everything you do or buy together.

ANNA'S STORY...

Money caused more rows than anything else in Anna and Richie's stormy relationship. After he moved in with her he refused to pay his way, arguing that she'd be paying the rent and bills whether he was there or not. After Anna finally threw him out, it was payback time. Unable to recoup her losses in any other way, she got a court to agree he should make monthly maintenance payments toward the cost of keeping the cat they had bought together. Meow!

Wherever you're both coming from, you'll find if you're honest about your attitudes to money and your money-management skills from early on, there'll be less need to argue.

CALLING EACH OTHER TO ACCOUNT

No need to treat this like an interview with the bank manager. All of the questions opposite will help you to get the measure of each other and can be slipped into a conversation (now that you've learned how to get him talking!). You never know, you might even have fun discovering whether you're money-made for each other, or in fact money-miles apart. Ask yourselves the following questions and answer them truthfully and independently. Try not to be influenced by his answers when you are thinking about your own.

FINANCIAL CHECK UP

1 *If you lost your job, which three things would you no longer spend money on?*

2 *If you won the lottery, what would you do with the money?*

3 *Do you like to have savings?*

4 *If so, what are you saving for?*

5 *How many credit cards do you have?*

6 *Is it OK to have debt? Is it OK to overdraw your account?*

7 *Do you know how much money is in your current account at any time?*

8 *If you were your boss, how much would you pay you (honestly)?*

9 *Do you budget each month to make sure you live within your means?*

CREDIT CONTROL

Financial acumen isn't just about understanding money and how it works, but also about understanding him—and how that will help you to hit the jackpot now and then.

With a bit of luck, working through your feelings about money, understanding his side of the story, and being honest with each other will add up to complete cash compatibility. No relationship built on deceit will have staying power. But there's no harm using what you know about his money make-up to ensure that you're sometimes ahead of the game.

REAPING RICH REWARDS

1 *You know he hates shopping. All you have to do is pretend to hate it too, but hey, someone's got to do it. He'll be so grateful you volunteered he'll be happy to hand over his credit card.*

2 *The competitive streak in him can't help wanting to keep up with the Jones/ Jacksons/Jaipurs. Enlist your friends' help in spreading the word about the gorgeous jewelry/car/house someone else's partner has bought for them. Remember Chloe and her sports car? No kidding—soon after that party, two of the guys who'd been there bought cars for their girls.*

3 *Think of your spending as an investment in you both. You're spending for two! After all, that lovely designer lingerie you bought may have been expensive, but it should delight him every bit as much as you.*

4 *Get political. The whole of the Western economy depends on people continuing to spend money. If he challenges you, point out you're simply doing your bit to keep the wheels of commerce grinding on, and him in a job.*

THAT'S

MAN'S WORK!

IT STARTED WITH CINDERELLA AND SNOW WHITE. THERE WE WERE, IMPRESSIONABLE LITTLE GIRLS, AND THE BEST ROLE MODELS THAT THE ADULT WORLD COULD SERVE UP TO US WERE A PAIR OF LADIES OBSESSED WITH HOUSE- HOLD CHORES. CINDERELLA MAY HAVE GOT HER PRINCE IN THE END (AND IT'S A SAFE BET THAT HE NEVER LIFTED A FINGER TO HELP AROUND THE PALACE). BUT HOW DID SHE PROVE SHE WAS WORTHY OF A HAPPY ENDING? BY DOING EVERY TINY THING AROUND HER STEPMOTHER'S HOUSE, AND NEVER ONCE COMPLAINING, THAT'S HOW. AS FOR SNOW WHITE, THE POOR GIRL HAD TO COOK AND CLEAN FOR NO FEWER THAN SEVEN LITTLE GUYS BEFORE SHE EARNED THE RIGHT TO BE RESCUED FROM HER LIFE OF DRUDGERY.

IT'S TIME TO CHANGE THE STORY, GIRLS!

We've already looked at how women are wired to please. Which is certain to get in the way of arranging a fair division of labor in your relationship.

Try this quiz to see whether you've got what it takes to sweep away all that conditioning—and watch as he sweeps the carpet.

DRUDGE OR DIVA?

When it comes to love, you'll get further working at your relationship than you ever will working around the house.

SOUNDS FAMILIAR?

It's his turn to clean the shower but you've already stripped before you notice two furry animals seem to have had a fight in the soap dish. Do you:

a *Furiously grab the cloth and attack the filth, swearing loudly while wishing it was his sensitive parts you're ruthlessly scrubbing, and rehearsing the dressing down he's going to get.*

b *Abandon your plans for a shower. While you're cleaning up the bathroom you may as well do the rest of the place. You can clean yourself up later.*

c *Wander tantalizngly naked into the living room and point out his omission. Watch him snap to attention. He may even decide to join you in the shower.*

You've got a pre-dawn start in the morning and realize you've forgotten to fill up with fuel. There's a gale outside but if you don't gas up tonight you'll have to get up even earlier the next day. Do you?

a Blame him. Cars are a guy's responsibility. You make sure he knows you're upset by needling him all evening, until he's so exasperated that he opts for a quiet life and goes out to gas up your car for you.

b Sigh deeply and resign yourself to setting the alarm 15 minutes earlier. You've still got a load of ironing to do, and dinner to cook, and the evening's already half over.

c Ask for his help, explaining you've forgotten about the car and still have plenty to do before you can get to bed for some much needed sleep.

GETTING HIM INVOLVED REQUIRES MORE EFFORT THAN SIMPLY TELLING HIM WHAT TO DO—HE'LL RESIST. DON'T DO IT ALL YOURSELF EITHER! TACTICAL MANEUVERING IS CALLED FOR...

DRUDGE OR DIVA? CONTINUED

He's offered to cook Thanksgiving dinner but you can sense the only thing on the menu is a culinary disaster. He's burned the bird and seriously misjudged the quantities for pumpkin pie which is oozing all over the oven like volcanic lava. Do you:

a Point out his mistakes loudly and demand to know whether he's deliberately sabotaged dinner. Say—or yell—that next time you'll just do it yourself.

b Shepherd him out of the kitchen, roll up your sleeves, and try to salvage what you can. All your suspicions that it's quicker and less problematic to do things yourself have been confirmed.

c Stay exactly where you are, in front of the fire with a glass of wine, resolving that he's old enough to work out where he's gone wrong, but he'll never get better if you don't allow him plenty of practice.

Mostly a)s You're so uncomfortable about sharing the chores you're in danger of turning your home into a battleground. You want him to do his fair share but you want him to do it your way—and pay for all the guys who don't pull their weight. Seriously, you need to lighten up. Grown-up love is about collaboration, not competition. **Mostly b)s** Cinderella is alive and well in your home. Deep down you still believe it's all women's work, and he'll go along with that because he hates to disappoint you. There are slicker ways of showing you love him than shining the porch floor. Loving yourself enough to insist you share the chores, for instance! **Mostly c)s** You don't need anyone to tell you that real life and love are all about giving and taking. And you're as comfortable with one as the other. Go straight to the top of the class.

103

HOME FROM HOME

Unless the two of you live in a palace with servants to take care of things, you'd do well to find out whether your Prince Charming is able to look after himself.

Unless you scored all c)s in the last section you really do need to give your attitudes a spring clean. You're both adults, you've probably both got jobs, you both make a mess (chances are, if his hobbies include contact sport, he makes a lot more than you). Why should you draw the short straw when it comes to dividing the household labor?

If you come from the sort of home where your dad gave your mom a new vacuum cleaner or saucepan set for Christmas, then you may have a little further to come.

Unfortunately, the same is true of him. If you're really lucky, he'll have been born in the seventies, to a woman who read feminist magazines while she was in labor and taught him how to wash the dishes even before she taught him to wash behind his ears.

But the odds are far greater that his mom's willingness to do everything except blow his nose for him (and she only stopped doing that when he graduated from high school) has left you with a huge challenge to make him do his share of housework.

HOW'S HIS HOUSE?

Long before you get serious you should do your homework. Get him to invite you to meet his parents and see if they treat him as top dog or dogsbody. Do some detective work at his place while he's not looking:

1 *What's the use-by date on the things in his cupboard?*

2 *Is the lid on the toothpaste?*

3 *When you open the closet, do his sneakers crawl out by themselves?*

He may well be worth the effort you're going to have to put in to get him house-trained. But it's a good idea to be wise to the true size of the task ahead.

The quickest way to getting help around the house is to give him the chance to act true to type.

WHAT TYPE IS HE?

PLAY THE GADGET GAME...

a You want him to do the vacuuming? Then invest in a bagless cleaner. Guys are fascinated by the science behind a machine that seems to make dust vanish. And don't forget the attractions of big, powerful engines. You could even point out that, like the motorbike he lusts after, this machine is too hot for you to handle (ha!)

b Fancy a break from cooking? Then splash out on an all-singing, all-dancing food processor. Not even construction kits match the high he'll get trying to figure out how the zillion pieces fit together, and once he's discovered how to mince lamb steaks into submission he might as well finish up the meal while you take a break.

c Paintwork looking a little tired? Treat him to a trip to the home improvement store and watch him salivate over all the dinky gadgets now available for stripping and applying paint and paper.

Like all the other areas of life and love we've looked at, getting his co-operation around the home is really only a question of understanding his male make-up. Luckily, the things that get your man hot are a perfect starting point for turning traditional male and female roles on their heads. Hopefully, your guy will have a helpful proportion of each of these types inside him:

GADGET MAN

Gadget man is God's gift to divas. His parents knew how to keep him quiet for hours with a Transformer or a box of Legos. All you have to do is find a grown-up equivalent to his boys' toys that can be put to good use around the home. The ideas above will give you a start, but you'll have to be guided by your guy's particular pets.

107

PREHISTORIC MAN

His ancestral past is alive and well in his DNA and you can trigger it any time. But take care that in harking back to prehistory you don't catapult yourself back to that cave where it was your job to keep the home fires burning. There's no rule that says only guys can hunt: go hunt those bargains out at the mall!

WHAT TYPE IS HE? CONTINUED

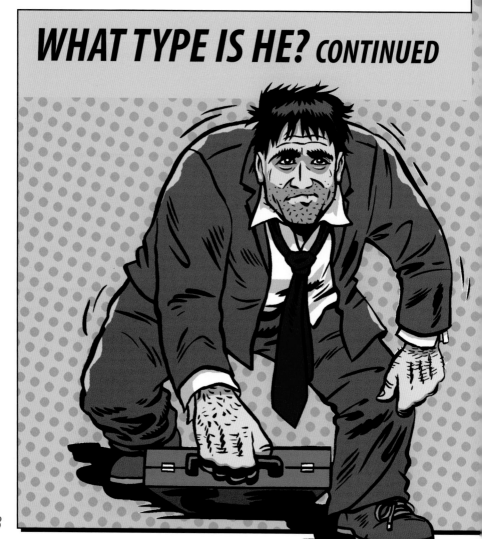

PLAY TO HIS INSTINCTS...

a Want a break from the kitchen? Suggest a barbecue. Guys and fires go together like girls and shoes. He sees building and tending a fire as the ultimate test of his masculinity. No need to reveal to him that Cinderella also knew how to make a mean fire. Sit back and let him make a wonderful outdoor meal.

b Bored of the supermarket run? There may be few opportunities for spearing, shooting, and fishing in your neighborhood, but deep down he still wants to bring home a bison, so give him the chance to rediscover the hunter inside by searching out some new delicacy at an out-of-the-way store. Mention you've heard of a neat place that's selling kangaroo steak or yak chops at the deli and watch him grab his car keys as though they were a bow and arrows.

c He just can't shake that competitive streak can he, even when it comes to something as mundane as cleaning the john? Make sure he's watching when they advertise that fantastic new product that leaves toilet bowls whiter than a dentist's teeth. It'll show up (with him) in the bathroom a few days later—only fair, as he spends many more hours than you getting up close and personal with the porcelain.

TECHNO MAN

There's a reason why guys are the biggest buyers of games consoles, and users of computers. They just love pushing back the technology frontiers, boldly going where no man except Bill Gates has gone before. Every time he explains, again, how a machine works, he's playing right into your hands.

WHAT TYPE IS HE? CONTINUED

PRESSING HIS BUTTONS...

a Want him to do the laundry? Make sure the front of your washing machine looks like the cockpit of a jet fighter. The more flashing lights, knobs, bells, and whistles it has, the more seductive he'll find its company. If the machine comes with a 200-page manual setting out the 70 stages to washing your underwear, so much the better.

b These days, there's almost nothing you can't do or buy on the Internet. Naturally you don't want to give up your shopping trips, but you won't miss carrying fruit, veg, light bulbs, kitchen roll and the rest home, so, while he's camped out on the computer, let him sort the boring shopping. And while he's at it, he can settle up all the utility bills online.

c Prefer to kick back and study the scenery when the pair of you are out somewhere? Then make sure your car comes with a satellite navigation system. Not only will he always volunteer to drive (even when you're off to a bar and one of you needs to abstain), there'll be no more fights about his pig-headed refusal to ask for directions, even though you'd swear you've been around the same block six times.

WHAT TYPE IS HE? CONTINUED

MR FIX IT

Imagine the scene, 10,000 years ago. He and his friends are all trying to work out how to turn a pile of twigs and a few animal skins into a shelter. Or how to attach a stone flint to a pole in order to develop an efficient hunting weapon.

THE HANDS-ON GAME...

He loves working out how to use things, how to fix things, and, if the thing doesn't exist, he loves inventing it. The last thing you want to do is spoil his fun by picking up the phonebook and calling the repair man.

a *Your car's making a funny noise and you've no idea what's wrong. Letting him loose under the hood with his toolkit is like letting a horse loose in a field of clover. While the engine's in pieces on the garage floor don't forget to mention it's due a service and the oil and filters are right there...*

b *Anything you want doing—get him the appropriate tool (it doesn't have to get expensive; pool together with your girlfriends and have it for a week each). He can't resist trying out any new toy, whether it's a whizzy drill or a glamorous garlic press.*

c *Alternatively, turn the thing you need doing into a puzzle. The plumbing's packed up and you don't know the difference between a ballcock and a ballboy, or where along the tangle of ancient pipes the problem actually lies. He'll treat the challenge like a complex mathematical puzzle and the only involvement he'll want from you is to listen intelligently each time he's able to report success. The more scope there is for him to prove his ingenuity and know-how to you, the better.*

Once you realize that tackling tasks is his way of proving he cares for you, you'll want to acknowledge the things he does for love.

A LABOR OF LOVE

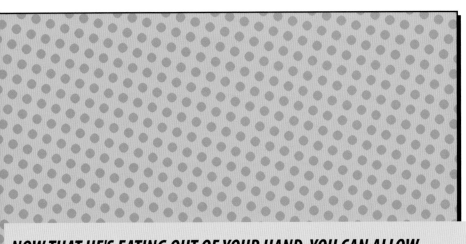

NOW THAT HE'S EATING OUT OF YOUR HAND, YOU CAN ALLOW YOURSELF A WRY SMILE. BUT DON'T GET CARRIED AWAY—YOU MUST SHOW YOUR GENUINE APPRECIATION FOR HIS EFFORTS.

For there's the key to it all: he clearly adores you but he's infinitely more comfortable proving his love practically. Actions really do speak much louder than words as far as he's concerned—especially when you're so much better at stringing a sentence together.

Understanding the way he ticks in order to get the work done is fine. But you owe it to him to notice what he's doing and, in return, give him back the things he wants from you: appreciation, admiration, and approval.

Back to one of the lessons we learned earlier. We all want to be respected, admired, and appreciated by the people we care about, the people whose opinions count for us. Make sure he knows how much you value the effort he makes around the house: he might even start to take more notice of the things you do for him!

If you're ever tempted to take his efforts to please you with a pinch of salt, think how you feel all those times the guys in your life (not to mention the friends, colleagues, or your boss) take you for granted.

It's a great feeling to know you've been useful. And it makes a huge difference when someone bothers to acknowledge your efforts—such a difference that you don't mind doing more. Nor will he…

Who does what isn't important, as long as you both agree you're doing your fair share around the home, and nobody feels like a martyr.

DARE NOT TO DUST

So where does that leave you while your guy's up to his ears? Lying on the couch with a glossy magazine, or holed up in the bathroom up to your ears in expensive bubble bath?

Probably not because, as we've said, your love's never going to outlast the latest fashion if one of you already feels you are taken for granted, overlooked, or exploited.

All you're aiming for is a division of labor that feels fair to you both. It doesn't matter if you decide he belongs in the kitchen and you belong in the tool shed (or both of you in the bedroom, leaving the local takeout to take the strain for keeping you fed). As long as the arrangement works for you, and you both remember never to take

the other's efforts for granted, you shouldn't go far wrong.

And while you're working it out between you, remember that if you do occasionally find a tidemark around the bath it's not like someone died.

Tackling the housework together with the music cranked up loud is all well and good. But what about the fun you could be having with your guy which doesn't involve dusters or dishcloths or dazzling kitchen surfaces? Very few people use their last breath to tell the world they wish they'd done more housework.

When you're gazing into each other's eyes you don't notice the dust. Pride in yourselves and each other will take you a lot further than being houseproud.

MAY'S STORY...

During their 40-year marriage, May's husband Stan did almost everything around the home: cooking, cleaning, shopping, gardening, and chauffeuring their two sons to school, play dates, and Little League. Far from his feeling hard done by, it was obvious to everyone who knew them that Stan and May really had found their perfect partners, and had a perfect relationship. The more Stan did for May, the more deeply she loved and appreciated him, and the more he wanted to do for her.

THE X FACTOR

You can go a long way with management training programs—but every training program naturally has its limitations.

In the end, whether your enterprise succeeds or fails will depend on the commitment of you and your partner to each other, rather than to the program. Book learning can take you only so far—as any girl who's been on the receiving end of a guy whose bedroom technique has come straight from a sex manual can testify!

And while it's helpful to draw comparisons with what proper training can achieve in the world of work, there are also some important differences.

In the workplace you might pour your heart and soul into your job, working 25 hours a day, signing up for every training course on offer—and despite that effort, you might still not be up to the job that needs doing. In which case your company is going to wave you goodbye.

Where love's concerned your guy may be failing dismally, or making no effort, but deep down you don't want to show him the door. After all, if we were able to faultlessly control our hearts we'd never ever fall for anyone less-than-perfect (for us) in the first place. For all his faults, you recognize that you and he together have the X factor and for that you'll forgive him a great deal.

Even if he seems a hopeless case, all is not lost. There may be good reasons why your man-management program is not working.

GUYS BEHAVING BADLY

Why is your man management training failing with your guy?

Maybe his skull really is denser than the earth's core, in which case you need to run and re-run your program until he begins to understand.

Other factors that may be getting in the way of him learning anything include his ego. Perhaps he's the type who just can't comprehend that anything about him might need changing. He's the know-it-all at the front of the class who ruins it for everyone else by refusing to co-operate (or listen), too busy making cynical comments, and pointing out where you're going wrong, to learn anything.

Or he's got you mixed up with his mother, his old school, his boss. Far from seeing you as a partner, trying to build a better relationship, you're a figure of authority—and he's reacting like a naughty boy sitting in the back row, sabotaging your attempts to build a better relationship with inattention, pranks, and disrespect. He definitely needs to grow up.

Before you throw the rulebook at him, consider whether there are extenuating circumstances. If he's always been made to feel he's not good enough, then any hint that you want him to change will send a defensive knee jerking right into the center of your plans.

Or perhaps his background or the influence of his peers mean he has further to travel than other guys to achieve a satisfactory mark. Take a look back to chapter four to remind yourself he needs building up as well as training.

The other thing to consider is whether he's not the only one who has a little learning to do. Are you certain you understand your own motivations? Without meaning to we sometimes set people up to fail because what we say we want isn't what we're really looking for. Take a look (above) at a few of the traps we lay for those we love and make sure you understand yourself as well as you want him to understand you.

If none of these things apply to either of you then you are going to have to face the possibility that he's not the guy you thought he was. He may simply not be grown up enough to be part of an adult, equal relationship.

This is the point where, like any manager, you need to step back and ask yourself whether he's really the right guy for you. Exactly how far are you willing to compromise? Is he worth it? Are the feelings you have for him stronger than his shortcomings, or likely to be undermined by your doubts?

CONDUCTING AN APPRAISAL

Relationships flounder for all sorts of reasons—you need to figure out what you can live with, and what you can't.

However good a trainer you are, you won't succeed in every area. The trick is to sort out your priorities and decide how well he measures up to them.

Maybe he's not great at the sort of gossipy sessions you enjoy with your girlfriends. But since you've got them, do you need him to be? On the other hand, he knows just when paying a fantastic compliment will lift your mood and your self-esteem on the worst of bad hair days. Which things

When Jane broke up with Kevin she told her friends it was because he never cleaned the bathroom after he'd used it.

Millions of relationships break up over such silly little things—except of course they're not silly at all. They're symptomatic. Jane probably could have learned to live with the black rings (she might even have dreamed up an imaginative way to get him back such as shaving her legs with his expensive razor) if she'd felt loved, cherished, and heard by Kevin in other ways.

But it was like living with a little boy who only ever focused on his own needs, and put hers somewhere beneath the washcloth he refused to pick up. Kevin didn't care enough about pleasing Jane to change something which, for whatever reason, was really important to her.

1 Lock yourself away somewhere quiet and on a blank piece of paper draw three columns. Label them "hit list," "prospects," and "outlook."

2 Under "hit list" write down all the things he does—or doesn't do—that annoy, upset, or disappoint you. It could be something as mundane as forgetting to put the milk back into the cooler, or as huge as criticizing the way you look. What you're after is a comprehensive list of all those areas where there's potential for a fight—or a break-up.

3 Now work through those items one by one and alongside each note whether you think there's a realistic possibility that his behavior could change. Might your training program work or is this aspect of his behavior as much a part of his make-up as the color of his eyes or his shoe size?

4 Finally, go through the list again, focusing only on those items where you've predicted "no change." Write down the feeling each of these items produces in you: exasperation, reluctant acceptance? Or sadness, anger, despair? By identifying your emotional response you'll begin to see whether you have got a future together. Can you live with him? Do you want to, if it means you'll still be feeling this sad about his behavior in 10 years' time?

matter the most to you? Make your life richer, funnier, happier, more loving? How does he measure up against those?

Conduct an appraisal by following the steps above. But remember every relationship has its moments of anger, frustration, annoyance, and unhappiness—especially those that involve living with someone.

Most of us don't lose our jobs for the occasional slip-up, for the days when we under-perform or are mildly irritating to our colleagues. On the other hand, there are things that might warrant instant dismissal. If the appraisal produces powerful negative feelings, is it time to ask yourself if you've reached the parting of the ways?

PERFECT PARTNERSHIPS

There's one other important difference in your approach to man management in the office and in your love life.

Let's face it, as supportive as your boss is, it's unlikely he or she actually wants you to become so brilliant at your job that you take over theirs. They may be an excellent manager but you're both there to do a good job for the organization, rather than each other.

Whereas you care enough about your guy to want to make it work. Why else would you invest in training him?

In which case you need to remember at every stage along the way that, unlike the world of work, your aim is to make him into your perfect partner. Not a subordinate, even if you have to go on managing him for the rest of the time you are together. But a full and equal partner in the enterprise.

If this is all about your goals you may fool him into thinking he wants what you want. But this will only last as long as it takes to dawn on him that you are working solely to your own agenda.

Just look at the way politicians fall out when their interests no longer match those of their allies. Loyalties vanish and everyone looks for a new partner.

Compared to politics, the basis of your relationship is blissfully simple: you're aiming to create a strong, honest, nurturing relationship, in which you both give and get what you need.

And enjoy the giving and getting in equal measure because of the way you feel about each other.

Now go clinch the deal!

INDEX

Acknowledgments

Illustrations on pp. 14–15, 40, 44, 48, 51, 52, 59, 61. 65, 68, 73, 81, 85, 93, 96, 105, 108, 110, 112, 117, 127, 128 by Keith Sparrow